iPhone 15 M

I0021442

Unlock the Ultimate iphone 15 pro max Experience with
an Illustrative Beginners Comprehensive iPhone 15 Pro
User Guide Book!

Chris Amber

Table of Contents

One of the most anticipated updates to the iPhone in a long time is the action

PREFACE

Discover the Full Potential of Your iPhone 15 with Our Detailed User Guide Book!

Are you prepared to enhance your iPhone 15 experience further? There's nowhere else to look! Our unique user guide book is made to improve your iPhone skills and serve readers worldwide.

Inside:

- Thorough explanation of the features and capabilities of the iphone 15.

- Advice on how to get the most out of your gadget.

- Detailed instructions for learning how to use the newest iOS releases.

- Discover the possibilities of state-of-the-art technology at your fingertips!

Why Select Our User Manual?

- *Worldwid4e Reach:* Our guide is ideal for people

everywhere because it is not limited by language.

- *User-friendly:* Our tutorial is designed for all levels of experience, from novices to IT enthusiasts.

- *Visually captivating:* Rich with eye-catching pictures and graphics that make understanding simple.

- *Regular upgrades:* Keep up with the most recent improvements and upgrades for the iphone 15.

⊕ **Go Beyond Your iPhone 15 with These Handpicked Suggestions:**

- *Samsung S23:* Experience Android with the newest innovation from Samsung.

- ☑ *Unlock iPhone XS and iPhone XR* to explore an infinite array of options by selecting your own carrier.

- 🛡 *Privacy Screen Protector for iPhone 14 Pro:* Protect your privacy with cutting-edge safeguards.

- 💼 *For the best possible device protection*, combine style and durability with the Spigen iPhone 14 Pro Max Case.

- 🪁 ***Unlocked iPhone 13 Pro Max:*** Unrestrictedly use the full capability of your iPhone 13!

🌼 Adorn and Safeguard:

- ***Spigen iPhone 14 Pro Case:*** Up your style game with this stylish case.

- 🛡 ***Protector Para iPhone 14 Pro Max:*** We've got you covered if you speak Spanish! 🔒

- ***iPhone 14 Plus Privacy Screen:*** Protect your screen from snoopers.

🔒 Activate a Universe of Opportunities:

- ***Unlocked iPhone 11 Pro Max:*** Unrestricted access to global networks.

- 🪁 ***Boost Infinite:*** Enhance your iPhone experience and increase connectivity.

↩ *Grow Your Apple Network:*

- 🍎 *Apple Watch:* For a connected lifestyle, seamlessly integrate your wearable technology.

- 📺 *Apple TV:* Upgrade your viewing pleasure with the company's newest TV innovation.

Upgrading to the iPhone 15 and Later:

- 📱 iPhone 14, iPhone SE, iPhone 13, iPhone 13 Mini Unlocked: Keep up with the newest iPhone models to stay technologically advanced.

- 🌼 Take in the ultimate Apple experience with the Apple Max.

📞 Get Your Copy Now to Explore the Next Frontier of iPhone Technology! 🚀 📚

Get in quick, while supplies last! Globally accessible. 🎇

INTRODUCTION

Get an iPhone 15 but also a handbook that teaches you how to make the most of all of its amazing features. If you settle for anything less, you won't be able to fully utilize this incredible smartphone.

Get ready for the next wave of smartphone innovation. The much anticipated iPhone 15 is about to change how we use our phones. Modern features and technology are anticipated to make the iPhone 15 the most cutting-edge and inventive smartphone to date. With its improved camera features and longer battery life (Which help you not to carry Power Banks around), the iPhone 15 is expected to have a big impact on the mobile device market.

Presenting the much awaited iPhone 15! With its most recent release, which is jam-packed with cutting-edge features and technology, Apple has lifted the bar once more. With its sophisticated camera features, improved performance, and stylish new appearance, the iPhone 15 has raised the bar for smartphones.

"iPhone 15 Manual" is a guidebook written with the inexperienced user in mind, not just a handbook. Our goal is to demystify each feature and convey it in an easy-to-understand manner. We'll walk you through exploring the technological wonders of your smartphone using simple language and clear visuals, making the learning experience entertaining as well as instructive.

Discover how to use your iPhone's amazing cameras to capture incredibly gorgeous images and movies.

With its remarkable assortment of seven professional-grade lenses, 48MP Main camera, new camera modes, astounding 24MP default resolution, special 5x Telephoto camera, and numerous other new camera capabilities, the new iPhone 15 series camera is brimming with never-before-seen features on a smartphone.

This extensive user manual explores all of the capabilities that make use of the iPhone camera, including the FaceTime, Photos, and Camera apps. You'll learn how to unleash your creative potential by learning how to position and adjust your camera for the perfect picture and video capture.

This book aims to provide you comfort, familiarity, and comprehension with your device so that you can explore with confidence rather than overwhelming you with technical terms or cliches.

Explore the world of apps in great detail, learn the meaning behind features, and master the iPhone 15. The pictorial guide will not only pique your curiosity but also inspire you to discover and utilize the cutting-edge capabilities of your gadget, which will make daily chores more enjoyable and effective. This guide covers everything, from configuring your new iPhone to comprehending the settings, making the most of the camera, and protecting your security and privacy. The icing on the cake are the extra tips and tricks that guarantee you are making the most of your iPhone hassle-free.

Enjoy your new iPhone 15 to the fullest and don't let your fear of technology get in the way! Take a deep dive into this thorough and detailed guide to master your gadget.

A few of the topics this manual covers are as follows:

- The iPhone 15 & 15 Plus's components

- The LiDAR Scanner's operation

- Establishment Process

- iCloud Profile

- How to Utilize the Phone Locator Feature

- Introducing the features of iOS 17

- Discover the iPhone 15 Series' innovative photography features.

- Discover the techniques for taking breathtaking images in low light and extending your dynamic range using Smart HDR and Night mode.

- Learn the techniques of expert photo editing to create truly amazing images from your photos.

- With the help of cutting-edge Depth and Control Focus technology, your portrait photography will soar.

- How to initialize your Apple Pay account

- How to use Apple Pay with a credit or debit card

- How to make contactless payments with Apple Pay

- How to locate locations that use Apple Pay using Siri

- How a gift card is used

- How to use Safari's Apple Pay feature

- Crucial Elements in the Entire Series: Examine the unique qualities that make the iPhone 15 series unique.

- File Transfer from Android to iPhone 15: Ensure a seamless and trouble-free move.

- Using Picture-in-Picture mode to multitask can increase productivity.

- Sync your data between devices with ease by using the iCloud Settings.

- Activate this function by using the Action Button.

- Aligning Camera Shooting Angle: Sharpen your photographic techniques to produce jaw-dropping images.

- Use Night Shift to lessen eye strain and enhance the quality of your sleep.

- Configuring and Personalizing Siri: Customize Siri to meet your needs!...and our guide has a lot more in store for you!

Don't allow doubt stop you from using your smartphone to its fullest capacity. Stay tuned for more information on this exciting new product's debut and upgrades. Continue reading to get all the fascinating specifics of this revolutionary gadget.

CHAPTER 1

News, Specs, Price, and Release Date for the iPhone 15

The iPhone 15 was revealed on September 12, 2023. Preorders are accepted right now, and shipping begins on September 22. Numerous updates have been made to this edition, including the switch to USB-C, the addition of an Action button reminiscent of the Apple Watch, slimmer bezels, Dynamic Island for all versions, and titanium Pro variants.

Features of the iPhone 15 and 15 Plus

The iPhone 15 is offered in four versions, like it did last year: iPhone 15, 15 Plus, 15 Pro, and 15 Pro Max. The screens on the 15 and Pro are 6.1 inches, while the screens on the Plus and Pro Max are 6.7 inches.

There are tons of amazing features and options in the new iPhone 15 series. Here are a few noteworthy ones that

Apple revealed at the launch event:

- A fresh layout featuring the Dynamic Island, which grows and changes in response to your actions. For instance, you can use it to simultaneously manage music, view instructions, and monitor deliveries and sports scores.

- Thinner boundaries and support for Dolby Vision.

- Extremely powerful A16 core CPU

- A GPU with five cores is great for graphics and games.

- Reaches a brightness of 1600 nits, reaching 2000 nits in direct sunlight.

- Resistance to water.

- 75% recyclable aluminum with 100% recycled copper foil.

- Completely new, cutting-edge camera system: a 48 megapixel primary camera and a 12 megapixel telephoto lens that provide high-resolution portrait possibilities and continuous zoom even in dim or dusk light.

- The iPhone 15 boasts an upgraded ultra-wideband with a second-generation chip that enhances precise position finding, ideal for locating loved ones.

- Speech Isolation: A machine learning algorithm that gives priority to your speech over other sounds, resulting in improved audio quality.

- SOS for emergencies: Extended to 14 nations across 3 continents.

- Roadside assistance with satellite: With AAA, you may get moving from anywhere at any time with a fast text that directs you to a satellite (needs AAA membership; free for two years with iPhone 15).

- USB-C connector for data transfer and charging. AirPods, iPad, iPhone, and Mac are all charged by this as well.

- To make it easier to align your phone with a

wireless charger, use MagSafe.

Features of the iPhone 15 Pro and Pro Max

All the features of the iPhone 15 are available on the iPhone 15 Pro/Pro+ models, but they go one step further:

- A17 Pro, the first 3-nanometer chip in the industry With microarchitectural and design advancements, the new CPU is up to 10% quicker, and the Neural Engine—which powers iOS 17's autocorrect and Personal Voice features—is now up to 2 times faster.

- Click the action button. This takes the role of the Mute/Silence switch, however it will still function as such by default. You may configure the Action Button to do a number of tasks, such as launching the camera app, initiating a shortcut, or even turning on the flashlight.

- A titanium design with recycled aluminum inside that employs grade 5 titanium, which is extraordinarily robust and durable but incredibly lightweight.

- The thinnest iPhone boundaries ever

- Available in 6.1" and 6.7" sizes.

- Four colors are possible with a PVD exterior coating: White, Black, Blue, and Natural (uncolored Titanium).

- An internal chassis architecture that makes it easy to repair the phone.

- ProMotion: The new, extremely high-resolution 24MP default capture is now supported by the 48MP main camera system. The system includes features including Night mode upgrades, Focus and

Depth Control for the next generation of portraiture, and Smart HDR.

- When the phone is on standby—which is a fully customizable experience—it is rotated horizontally and charges.

- Pro Performance: A brand-new A17 Pro chip made with a novel 3-nanometer manufacturing technique. Two high-performance cores and four high-efficiency cores make up the new A17 Pro's six core CPU. Now, the GPU has six cores.

- Ten gigabit per second (Gbps) of transfer speed is possible with a USB-C connector and a USB 3 controller (20 times faster than prior generations).

- Energy-efficient gaming features include hardware-based ray tracing to reflect gaming environments faster than ever (4 times faster), better resolution for higher-quality features, MetalFX scaling to provide more detailed gaming environments, and mesh shading for better graphics that use less power.

- Multiple lenses, the longest optical zoom ever with Focus and Depth Control, enhancements to Night mode and Smart HDR, and an entirely new 5x Telephoto camera available only on the iPhone 15 Pro Max comprise a pro camera system. This features a 5X mm telephoto camera with a 120 mm lens and a 12MP Ultra Wide camera with a 10x optical zoom capability.

- Ability to record spatial video for use on the Apple Vision Pro.

When Is the iPhone 15 Coming Out?

The iPhone 15 Pro and iPhone 15 Pro Max went on sale on Friday, September 22, and pre-orders started on September 15.

There will be four color options for the iPhone 15 Pro and iPhone 15 Pro Max: black, white, blue, and natural titanium.

Pricing of the iPhone 15 and iPhone 15 Pro

The iPhone 15 starts at $799, while the Plus starts at $899.

There are three different storage options: 128GB, 256GB, or 512GB.

There are four storage options for the iPhone 15 Pro: 128GB, 256GB, 512GB, and 1TB. It costs $999.

Starting at $1,199, the iPhone 15 Pro Max comes in three storage options: 256GB, 512GB, and 1TB.

With a new subscription, customers who buy the iPhone 15 Pro or iPhone 15 Pro Max will receive three months of free access to Apple Arcade and Apple Fitness+.

The Tetraprism Camera on the iPhone 15 Pro Max Is Another Typical Apple Surprise

One of the more clever revelations from Apple in recent memory is the new tetraprism 'zoom' lens seen in the iPhone 15 Pro Max. Apple excels at taking an established concept and turning it into something new.

Tetraprisms are similar to periscope lenses, however instead of spinning a long tube of lenses to run the length of the iPhone, they are formed by folding a prism into waves. It's a really clever concept that will increase the flexibility of the iPhone camera system.

"With an aperture of 2.8 and a focal length of 120mm, this lens is going to be a serious portrait lens. It will create real background blur, not the artificial kind that can look unnatural," replied travel photographer Tom Bourdon in an email interview with Lifewire. "I imagine many photographers will upgrade to this mobile simply because of this lens."

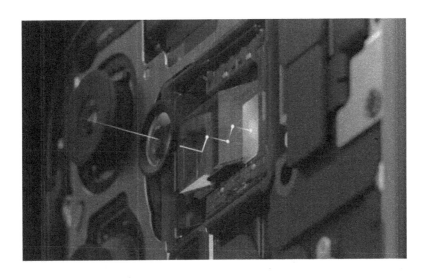

Go Live on Periscope

Periscope lens rumors have surrounded the iPhone for years, but now that it's official, it's even more intriguing than anticipated. Let's examine its necessity first, then move on to how it functions.

You may have seen the large camera turret protruding out the rear of a current iPhone Pro model if you have used one. It is there to support ever-larger lenses—which are required for the larger camera sensors—and to expand the iPhone's camera array's telephoto capabilities. However, as we can see, the turret is currently absurdly large and won't be able to become much bigger before being completely unusable.

A periscope lens is precisely what you would expect it to be. It runs the length of the iPhone rather than protruding perpendicularly from the back panel, allowing the lens to be longer. It does this by using prisms to reflect incoming light across a 90-degree angle. This design's drawback is that it requires more internal room in the camera.

Apple is applying the periscope concept without twisting it to a 90-degree angle. Rather, four links have been inserted into an internal prism, each of which folds light to make the light path longer while maintaining alignment with the other conventional lenses.

The fact that all of these kinks are contained within a

single tetraprism simplifies matters and might help explain why the lens appears to not absorb too much light, leading to that bright (at least for this focal length) maximum aperture of 2.8.

A glass prism can have exceptional optical quality. Pentaprisms, or glass blocks that reflect incoming light off five internal surfaces and bring it to your eye, are used in the viewfinders of high-quality SLR and DSLR cameras. The large angled viewfinder piece on top of the camera contains that.

iPhone Lens Reach

What then is the potential of a 120mm lens? The natural response is that the additional magnification allows you to get closer to the subject. Although you won't be able to select your child out of the entire cast of their upcoming school play, you can zoom in close to get rid of most of the distracting background.

This kind of long telephoto lens works well for portraiture as well. A subject appears more distorted in the frame the closer you approach to them. Get up close to someone else's face, close one eye, and observe how strange their features appear from this vantage point. Bulbous nose, receding cheeks, etc. Wide-angle lenses necessitate coming near to the subject, which is why they are so unattractive.

This is not the case with the telephoto lens. It enables you to take frame-filling pictures from a greater distance, resulting in far more attractive pictures. A subject is also naturally separated from everything behind them by a longer lens, which likewise blurs the background more than a wide lens does.

Additionally, the quality is far greater because there is no "digital zoom" involved—rather, the magnification is purely optical—rather than merely cropping the image to highlight the center.

Let's end with a rumor, since we began with one. The 15 Pro Max is currently the only iPhone with a tetraprism lens, but that will change the next year. If you're not like large phones, you can wait a year before replacing your phone if supply-chain sources claim that the standard iPhone 16 will gain this fantastic feature.

For many people, especially those who shoot a lot of pictures, this single-camera boost may be enough to justify purchasing a new phone. If not, wait, since this is most likely how iPhone cameras will look in the future.

The Potential Benefits of Ray Tracing for iPhone 15 Gamers

Soon, the next iPhone may mimic the functionality of a game console.

The latest A17 Pro chip, designed with improved GPU capabilities in mind, powers the iPhone 15 Pro. Apple asserts that the new 6-core design of this state-of-the-art "pro-class" GPU improves performance while simultaneously decreasing power consumption. By introducing hardware-accelerated ray tracing, the gadget claims to have GPU performance that is up to 20% quicker than before.

"Ray tracing provides better level design, better gameplay and, as a result—better user experience," said Pavel Shkarpenin, platform relations manager at MY.GAMES, in an email interview with Lifewire. "Apple has been saying for years that we can expect unprecedented quality and gameplay in our pocket—and to be able to bring an ultra-realistic feel to games through advanced lighting techniques like ray tracing means Apple can more effectively deliver on that promise."

Is That an Apple Game Phone?

Some of the AAA titles that will be available on the recently announced iPhone 15 Pro include Assassin's Creed Mirage, Resident Evil 4 Remake, Resident Evil Village, Death Stranding, and a slew of others. For an even better iPhone gaming experience, Apple boasted of major performance upgrades and the use of ray tracing.

"The combination of incredible iOS optimization and Apple silicon performance make new iPhones better for gaming than they ever have been before," stated Shkarpenin. "While we didn't see a 120Hz (or even 90Hz) refresh rate on the cheaper iPhone 15, their inclusion on the flagship 15 Pro and Max models make both of these exciting prospects."

In addition to the A17 Pro's revolutionary architecture and upscaling, Ray Tracing—a lighting method that adds an extra degree of realism to games—will be crucial, according to Shkarpenin.

"Mobile gaming relies heavily on the ability to be efficient because you are using your phone for other things, and you are not necessarily playing while connected to a power outlet every day, which degrades battery life," according to him.

Nate Amaral, branding and communications coordinator at gaming startup ExitLag, said in an email that the new A17 Pro processor, which is part of the Pro lineup on iPhone 15, has two primary improvements for gaming: two additional GPU cores and the integration of Apple's Neural Engine with the GPU. According to him, this indicates that Apple is following Nvidia's lead and seeking to improve performance and efficiency by utilizing the GPU's architecture.

"Heavy graphic games, like Asphalt 9 or Genshin Impact, will see not only better graphics but better performance and battery consumption, making the push into 60/120 frames per second in an iPhone 15 Pro / 15 Pro Max a feasible reality," according to him. "The new iPhone 15 GPU brings more quality of life for gamers all over the board."

In an email, Steve Athwal, managing director of The Big Phone Store, highlighted how the components of the A17 Pro chip will enhance its gaming powers.

"For gaming, the key components will be the GPU and NPU, as these work together to deliver processor-intensive gaming graphics quickly," according to him. The Neural engine replicates the functionality of DLSS on an Nvidia RTX graphics card by functioning as a 'upscaler' when playing games. This enables the GPU to 'upscale' images from lower resolutions to higher ones, and by playing the game at a lower native resolution, the GPU can function at a considerably faster speed.

What Lies Ahead for iPhones Video game

Improvements to iPhone gaming may be on the horizon. Amaral stated that the most intriguing potential is that Apple would likely introduce the new GPU Architecture,

Ray Tracing, and Upscaling for its M3 lineup, which uses the A/A Pro chip series.

"We can expect M3 Macs and iPads with even better graphics and GPU calculations, which, together with the industry's crescent adoption of ARM/Mobile architecture, paves the way for Apple to be a serious gaming competitor," according to him.

The new iPhone might be able to take on products like the Logitech G Cloud or Valve Steam Deck with its combination of a top-notch screen and a new chip. For the time being, though, Windows PCs will continue to have the largest selection of games available to serious gamers.

The New Spatial Videos on the iPhone 15 Pro Are a Fantastic Present for Your Future Self.

Using the Vision Pro augmented reality goggles, the iPhone 15 Pro can record stunning 3D footage. And it will alter your life—though gradually.

Those of you who own an iPhone may be familiar with

and fond of Live Photos, which record a short video clip—complete with audio—to accompany each photo. You might have Live Photos of friends and family members going back eight years, since these have been available since the iPhone 6S in 2015. If you want to remember the person's movements and voice from years ago, these are far more effective than a standard still image. The new spatial picture and video capabilities are going to make that seem a lot more genuine.

"Live Photos on the iPhone always did more than capture images for me—they captured moments," says Maxwell Bentley, CEO of Bentley Media and a video producer. Enjoying a brief video clip of my fiancée laughing as we take a photo together, a breathtaking sunset over the Atlanta cityscape, or vacation highlights is one of my favorite things to do when I browse back over my feed. I can't wait to see how far the iPhone 15's Spatial Video capability takes this.

I Appreciate the Recollections

Give this mental exercise a go if you've worked with Live Photos before. Bring to mind an experience from a very long time ago. Just before your little one figured out how to open the kitchen saucepan drawer, it may be their first few toddling steps. It may be a snapshot from your own youth, a picture of your first romantic partner, or even a house that you adored but no longer live in.

Imagine if those moments were captured in real-time through photos. Being able to see those individuals move would be amazing, wouldn't it? Remember what they sounded like? As far as those old enough to remember their formative years are concerned, that is precisely how it will play out.

This is heading somewhere, and you already know it. Envision now that these recollections are accessible in three dimensions. As a kid, you can sit on the floor beside yourself while wearing Apple's Vision Pro headset. Either a 3D spatial video or a still 3D image with rotating or otherwise adjustable viewpoints could be here. Just picture yourself reliving those magical experiences from your life in this way. I find that quite astounding.

The development of more advanced forms of immersive media, such as Apple's Vision Pro, holds great potential for the future of memory preservation and reliving. According to graphic designer and tech expert Sanef Safwan, "the potential for enriching our connection with memories is evident in these innovations," but whether or not this becomes the killer feature for the iPhone Vision Pro depends on individual preferences.

Social Media or Vision Pro?

When Apple presented a father video his kids playing together with the 3D cameras in the Vision Pro headset during the launch event, it was a rare PR gaffe. The internet thinks it was scary because the dystopic hat blocked dad from seeing his kids.

It is wonderful that the iPhone 15 Pro can now record spatial audio and video since, as everyone knows, a parent who is absorbed in their phone is far more in the here and now. Even if you won't be able to see it in 3D until the Vision Pro is available for purchase at an unknown future date, isn't $3,500 worth it for the memories it will preserve?

Besides being more convenient, capturing from a phone also begs the question of potential uses for the captures. Making a social media post about them is a very real option.

"Living through the memories again would be more exciting. It will be fascinating to observe the impact on video-sharing platforms like Instagram, YouTube, TikTok, and others. I'm even more thrilled about that! Envision yourself fully immersed in a mountaintop experience while viewing a hiking movie shot by your beloved photographer. "Nothing beats that," Asmita Kunwar, proprietor of a fashion line and an Instagram influencer, proudly revealed.

We have no guarantee that the Vision Pro will be successful or that its price will eventually fall to a level where we can purchase it. However, you ought to begin recording spatial memories without a doubt if you purchase a new iPhone 15 Pro. I mean, you never know. Consider it a wonderful present for the you of tomorrow.

Improved Low-Light Performance, Automatic Portrait Mode, and More Come Standard with the iPhone 15's Cameras

During its most recent Wonderlust event, Apple largely showcased the capabilities of the new iPhone 15 line's improved cameras, which are a significant improvement above what the firm gave on the iPhone 14.

The first noticeable change is the upgraded camera sensor from 12 megapixels on the previous generation to 48 megapixels on the new iPhone 15. Apple claims that the 24-megapixel photographs produced by the primary camera provide "incredible" picture quality without consuming excessive storage space. A 2x telephoto mode is also available by cropping the sensor's middle 12 megapixels. For the first time in Apple's more cheap handset series, the iPhone 15 and iPhone 15 Plus provide three levels of zoom—0.5x, 1x, and 2x. If you ever want to get every detail of a scene, you can switch to the dedicated wide-angle lens.

Improvements to Apple's computational photography software back up the new hardware. To get photos with bokeh effects, for example, you can utilize any camera app's regular Portrait Mode. The iPhone 15 can automatically take depth information when you tap on a topic, which it may then utilize to blur the background. After taking a picture, you can even change the focus. Apple also claims that Night Mode will have crisper details and more vibrant colors. The business has also improved its Smart HDR feature so that it can deal with illumination that isn't uniform.

The Pro and Max models of the iPhone 15 naturally have

all the improvements to the camera quality that were available on the iPhone 15 and more. Apple claims that its new flagships include seven professional lenses' worth of features. You may choose between a 24mm, 28mm, or 35mm lens with the 48-megapixel main camera on the iPhone 15 and 15 Pro Max. In addition, the new telephoto camera on both phones has a 5x optical zoom and a 120mm lens. Although it's not the most zoom-friendly feature on the market, it is the most ever supplied by Apple in a mobile device. The new tetraprism design on the iPhone 15 Pro and 15 Pro Max, according to the company, also includes its most advanced optical image stabilization capability.

The two phones will receive an update from Apple later this year that adds functionality for spatial video capturing. This feature will be useful when the company's Vision Pro headset arrives. You may pre-order any iPhone 15 starting on Friday, September 15, and then you can buy one in stores starting on September 22.

USB-C, Dynamic Island, 48MP, and Beautiful Colors Are Added to the iPhone 15

The iPhone with USB-C has arrived. Today during its 'Wonderlust' event in Cupertino, California, Apple revealed the iPhone 15. As anticipated, the business has shifted to using USB-C instead of its proprietary Lightning connector, and both of the new iPhone 15 versions use the new port. This implies that connecting the new iPhones to a variety of gadgets, such as Apple's MacBook computers, will be simpler for users. However, it also means outdated Lightning accessories won't operate with the iPhone 15 without an adaptor. Conveniently, the switch to USB-C ensures that the new iPhones abide by impending EU legislation aimed at reducing electronic waste.

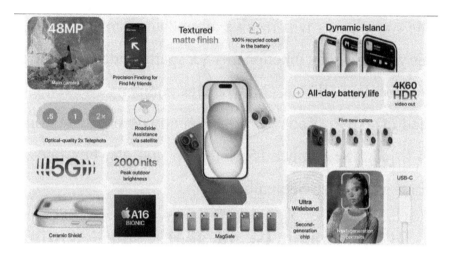

Similar to the iPhone 14 series, Apple will release the iPhone 15 in two sizes: 6.1 inches and 6.7 inches. The latter will continue to use the 'Plus' branding from the previous edition. The Dynamic Island display cutout, which Apple debuted in 2022, is new on the iPhone 15. That capability was limited to the iPhone 14 Pro and iPhone 14 Pro Max earlier.

Additionally, Apple fitted the iPhone 15 with a new Super Retina OLED screen, which has a brightness of 1,600 nits and can display HDR content. The new screen can reach a maximum brightness of 2,000 nits in sunny weather, which is twice as bright as the iPhone 14's display. The A16 Bionic technology, which Apple first unveiled with the iPhone 14 Pro last year, is also included with the two new iPhone 15 versions. With its most recent pair of mainstream smartphones, Apple is also boasting "all-day" battery life thanks to a larger battery.

Kaiann Drance
VP, iPhone Product Marketing

The iPhone 15 boasts a whole new primary camera array with a 12-megapixel telephoto lens and a 48-megapixel primary sensor for photographers. If it sounds similar, it's because Apple switched to the iPhone 14, which has a 48-megapixel camera. The iPhone 15's front camera features portrait lighting and autofocus for those who love taking selfies.

The new phones will be available from the company in a variety of vibrant colors, including Pink, Blue, Green, Yellow, and Black. This Friday, September 15, Apple will start taking preorders for the iPhone 15, with a September release date for wide availability. The iPhone 15 is priced starting at $799. Meanwhile, iPhone 15 Plus pricing will begin at $899.

Separately, Apple declared that on Monday, September 18, the upcoming iOS 17 version of its mobile operating system will be available as a free update. After revealing iOS 17 at its yearly WWDC conference in June, the Apple has been testing the new software in public. A number of new features will be included in the upgrade, such as a customizable call screen makeover and Check-In, which notifies reliable contacts when you've reached your location safely.

The iPhone 15 Pro's camera is more impressive than ever, but it still costs $999.

At its 'Wonder lust' event in California, Apple just unveiled the iPhone 15 Pro, which comes with a number of improvements.

With a revolutionary grade-five titanium construction, the iPhone 15 Pro weighs less than any previous iPhone model.

Apple says that because of a unique PVD coating, it's also their most durable phone to date. As previously, Apple will provide the Pro in two variants: a 6.1-inch model and a 6.7-inch 'Max' model. Additionally, the iPhone Pro's interior design has been altered by the business to increase its repairability and utilization of recycled materials. The iPhone 14 Pro has a new 'Action Button' in place of the previous ringer switch. The button can be configured by users to do specific functions. You may set up the button to start recording a voice memo, for example. It can also launch the camera app, activate the phone's flashlight, and do a lot more. Additionally, Apple is releasing a new standby display mode, which turns on when the phone is placed on a wireless charger in a landscape configuration.

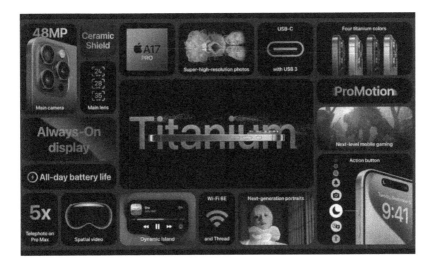

The new 3-nanometer A17 Pro chipset from Apple is housed inside the iPhone 15 Pro. The two high-performance cores on the new chip, according to the manufacturer, are 10% faster than those on the previous model. The integrated neural engine is also up to two times faster. In addition to being quicker, the GPU of the A17 Pro is capable of hardware-based ray tracing, which will enable game developers to include more lifelike lighting in their products.

While the A17 Pro has a specialized USB controller that allows 10Gbps data transfers, the iPhone 15 Pro also has USB-C connectivity. Naturally, Apple has also made significant updates to the iPhone 15 Pro's camera system. It boasts an upgraded 48-megapixel main camera that Apple claims is better at shooting low-light photographs and is less subject to lens flare (sorry, J.J. Abrams). Users of the camera can also alter the focus length. You may take pictures with focal lengths of 24 mm, 28 mm, and 35 mm. In addition, the telephoto camera comes with a 120mm focal length and an optical zoom of up to 5x.

Pre-orders for the iPhone 15 Pro and Pro Max will open on September 15. For the 128GB variant, the former starts at $999, while the latter starts at $1,119. On September 22, shipping will begin.

Separately, Apple declared that on Monday, September 18, the upcoming iOS 17 version of its mobile operating system will be available as a free update. After revealing iOS 17 at its yearly WWDC conference in June, the Apple has been testing the new software in public. A number of new features will be included in the upgrade, such as a customizable call screen makeover and Check-In, which notifies reliable contacts when you've reached your location safely.

CHAPTER 2

Practical Use Of the Apple iPhone 15 Pro

The A17 Pro chip, ultra-thin borders, Action button, USB-C port, Titanium finish, and iOS 17 out of the box are all features of the Apple iPhone 15 Pro. For the past week or so, I've been using the 15 Pro (1TB model) as my main smartphone, and aside from a little initial uncertainty (I'm more used to Android smartphones), I had a terrific experience.

Create and Present

Natural titanium, blue titanium, white titanium, and black titanium are the five colors available for the attractive and lightweight titanium smartphone known as the iPhone 15 Pro.

Slightly larger than the iPhone 14 Pro, the 6.1-inch display is covered with Ceramic Shield, a type of glass that, according to Apple, delivers four times the protection of rival smartphone glass.

It features Apple's Dynamic Island, which is a pill-shaped box at the top of the screen that shows notifications and running tasks (such timers or Map directions), just like the 14 Pro.

What's New?

The biggest modification is the move from Lightning to USB-C connectors for accessories and charging. You can also charge wirelessly with Qi-compatible chargers and Apple's MagSafe charging pad.

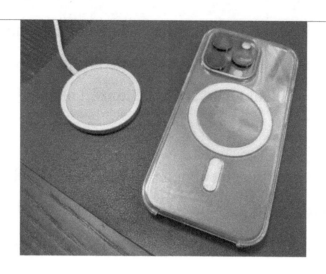

Additionally, the Action button added to the Pro model (which is still present on the iPhone 15 and 15 Plus) takes the place of the earlier models' Mute switch. It has the most recent Apple A17 Pro chip (as of 2023) installed.

Standby Mode, a new feature of iOS 17, allows you to use your lock screen to show a widget—like a huge clock—while it charges on your nightstand.

The iPhone 15, iPhone 15 Plus, iPhone 15 Pro, and the flagship iPhone 15 Pro Max are the four iterations of the iPhone 15 that Apple has launched.

Cameras, Features, and Performance

Even with numerous apps open, the iPhone 15 responds well and allows for fast app switching. FaceID was new to me, so I expected it to be difficult. (It's not an option on the Pro, but I prefer to use my fingerprint.) Fortunately, I was mistaken; without any effort at all, the screen unlocked at several angles right away.

I expect to see more development of the Action button, a cool new hardware feature, in next software releases. The phone goes into silent mode by default when the button, which is situated above the volume controls on the left side, is held down. That said, you can configure it to do a number of things, such as turning on your flashlight, recording a voice memo, and triggering a shortcut.

Instead of forcing you to choose only one action, I envisage future versions letting you select several (maybe with a short push or double press).

The iPhone 15 Pro has three cameras: a 3X zoom lens, an ultra-wide lens, and a 48MP primary camera. (The 5X periscope zoom lens on the 15 Pro Max.) It's a great addition that you can now utilize Portrait Mode on already-taken photographs. I will shortly add some examples to this review.

Undoubtedly remarkable, the iPhone 15 Pro is a smartphone that will not disappoint. It was the ideal size, in my opinion, to fit into a pocket and utilize with ease in one hand.

Specifications

Name of Product: iPhone 15 Pro;

Brand: Apple

Release Date: September 2023

Weight: 6.6 oz.

Product measurements: 2.78 by 5.77 by 0.32 inches.

The colors of titanium are natural, blue, white, and black.

Pricing begins at $999.

System: iOS 17 Processor

Apple A17 Pro Storage: 1TB (1TB tested), 256GB, 512GB, and 128GB

Primary 48MP telephoto, ultra wide, and camera system

Inputs/Outputs: USB-C

IP68 water resistance (waterproof up to 6 meters for 30 minutes)

What's Up Next for Wonderlust: The Release of the iPhone 15 and Much More

Fall is almost here, which means new iPhones. We're delving into leaks, speculations, and conjecture around the iPhone 15 today.

With nearly every aspect of the iPhone Pro remaining unaltered, some fantastic new hand-me-down capabilities for the standard iPhone, and a remote chance that Apple will release an even more costly iPhone above the Pro line, this year is looking to be a vintage year for new iPhone releases. The upcoming adjustments won't spare even the charging wires.

A Fall in Unexpected Expectations

First, on Tuesday, September 12, the iPhone 15 launch event is most likely scheduled. Unless there's a holiday or some other cause to deviate, Apple typically hosts events on Tuesdays. The iPhone event typically takes place during the second full week of September.

Apple just moved the iPhone to a new product cycle. Rather of replacing the same old processors in both the Pro and normal versions annually, the new processor is now only available in the iPhone Pro, while the conventional iPhone is left with last year's model. With a new three-nanometer chip technology that uses less energy and more power, the same is anticipated this year.

As for the standard, non-Pro iPhone, don't anticipate much. It will most likely receive the incredible Dynamic Island along with improved cameras, but that may be (almost— see below) it. To be honest, it's probably sufficient.

Let's talk about USB before moving on to the iPhone Pro and potential iPhone Ultra. The iPhone 15 will support USB-C data transfer and charging instead of Lightning. You won't have to worry about as many charging cables because this complies with EU regulation, which requires

USB-C charging on all new devices.

It's expected that Apple will also make available a new USB-C cover for the AirPods and AirPods Pro.

iPhone 15 Pro

Since we've previously discussed the potent new A17 chip, let's take a brief break to discuss the cameras within the new iPhone 15 Pro. The main speculation here is that the long-awaited periscope camera—yes, exactly what it sounds like—will be included in the XL-sized iPhone Pro Max. Instead than depending on ever-larger camera bumps to cram in bigger lenses, a periscope design flips the camera on its side so it may lay along the length of the phone instead of protruding out, utilizing optics to bend the incoming light through 90 degrees.

There will be much more alterations on the outside. First, since titanium is stronger, lighter, and maybe more flexible than steel, Apple may replace the steel band on the iPhone Pro. Because titanium can be anodized similarly to aluminum, additional colors for the Pro models should be anticipated. These will likely remain quite muted hues because, evidently, Pro models aren't able to appear stylish. Additionally, according to some speculations, the iPhone's back will have rounded corners to make it simpler to pocket.

And according to a [last-minute insider report], this titanium band will cut the weight of the pocket-dragging iPhone Pro model by roughly ten percent and switch to a brushed finish that won't show fingerprints like the existing smooth steel band. It's also about time, as up until now, the standard iPhone, which costs less, has an aluminum band that makes it better than the Pro model in both of these categories.

In addition, the mute switch on that titanium frame will most likely be replaced with a user-programmable action button, similar to the one seen on the Apple Watch Ultra.

I really enjoy the glanceability of the mute switch, but I also use my iPhone in silent mode almost all the time, so this one seems like a useful addition. For example, I could use it to turn on the camera and snap a picture.

Next, we have the screen itself, which will continue to be the same size yet grow larger. Of course, what we're talking about is reducing those bezels to accommodate a larger screen within the same body.

There's another reason why this year will be significant for the iPhone Pro. There have been rumors of an iPhone 15 Ultra. There's a chance that this is a completely new phone, but it could also be a rebranded version of Apple's dreadful iPhone Pro Max.

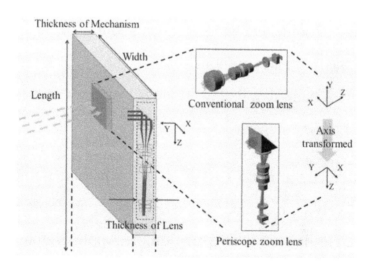

The forthcoming iOS, watchOS, and iPadOS releases will also be summarized by Apple.

In my opinion, the USB-C port on the iPhone and the periscope camera—should it ever arrive—will be the most intriguing features. Apple has been pleased with its exclusive Lighting connector and the license fees it can charge hardware manufacturers for its use for many years. It will be fascinating to watch the narrative Apple crafts to justify USB-C's superiority, all the while avoiding disparaging its own superb connector.

Even if there seem to be a lot of leaks and rumors, Apple has tightened up its privacy quite a bit in previous years, so there may be more surprises. I'll see you on September 12th!

Why the iPhone 15's USB-C port could be very important

Some experts are happy that Apple may finally be doing away with the Lightning connector in its upcoming iPhone.

Apple is getting ready to unveil its next generation of

gadgets this fall, and rumors have it that the top-tier iPhone 15 models will have a USB-C port among other noteworthy improvements. Some claim it's past overdue to abandon Lightning.

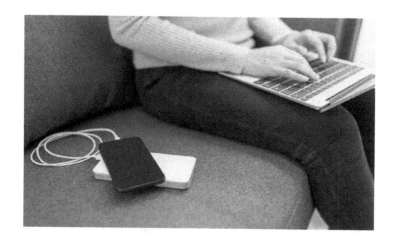

Tech expert Mark Vena said in an email interview that "USB-C is a universal standard embraced by various manufacturers, ensuring compatibility with a wide range of devices beyond Apple products." "Also, USB-C supports faster data transfer rates and higher power delivery, allowing for quicker charging and data syncing."

Finally, USB-C?

According to Vena, consumers would benefit from an iPhone with USB-C because of its simplicity and adaptability. Because of its reversible construction, plugging is simple and orientation is not a concern. Additionally, USB-C would do away with the need for numerous cables and adapters.

"Its compatibility with various devices makes it an essential connector for modern tech enthusiasts, simplifying connectivity and enhancing the overall user experience," he stated.

In an email, The Big Phone Store's managing director, Steven Athwal, pointed out that older USB ports, such mini and micro USB, had a lot of disadvantages. According to him, the amount of power and data that could be transferred using older USB ports was restricted and they were prone to breaking.

According to Athwal, Apple's in-house Lightning connector was a more dependable, quick, and robust option for iPhones prior to the release of USB-C. He pointed out that Lightning features an 8-pin, reversible, streamlined connector that can be placed either way up.

"Since the launch of USB-C, this connector has now become an almost universal standard for Android phones in a very short space of time—and these new connectors, which can transmit even more power and data than ever before, have fully caught up to Apple's Lightning connector in almost every way," he stated.

According to Athwal, USB-C can transport data more quickly than Lightning, which has a maximum bandwidth of less than 500Mbps. In addition, it comes with standard support for fast charging up to 100W, as opposed to Apple's 20W fast charging via its Lightning connectors at the moment.

However, abandoning Lightning has certain drawbacks.

According to Athwal, Apple is anticipated to go on with its "Made for iPhone" (MFi) certification program following the move to USB-C. Apple claims that by using software to verify the authenticity of the cable, customers can be shielded from having a subpar cable break their phone.

"However, despite your other USB-C cables having exactly the same connector, you won't necessarily be able to switch between them, and it's possible that users could become confused between which of their USB-C cables is iPhone-compatible," he stated. "This could cancel out the increased cross-compatibility you get by having one universal connector type."

Vena stated that the large selection of USB-C cables available on the market, each with a different quality level, would not always deliver the anticipated charging or data transmission speeds. It's possible that the modification will require you to buy new cables and adapters.

As stated in an email interview, "the main disadvantage is that users with Lightning accessories or cables will find them incompatible without an adapter," said Jason Wise, chief editor of the gadget website EarthWeb. "This might initially lead to some inconvenience and extra costs for users who have heavily invested in Lightning devices."

Numerous Improvements for the iPhone

There will be further updates added to the iPhone 15 lineup if the reports about USB-C turn out to be true.

One claim states that the iPhone 15 and iPhone 15 Plus would sport slightly larger displays, measuring 6.12 and 6.69 inches, respectively, owing to reduced bezels. They will also include Dynamic Island design and an A16 chipset. The upcoming iPhone 15 Pro and Pro Max models will have a state-of-the-art 3nm A17 CPU, ultra-thin bezels, a titanium chassis, an upgraded battery, WiFi 6E capability, and more RAM.

"Apple typically keeps its upcoming product details confidential until the official announcement," Vena stated. On the other hand, consumers may anticipate advancements in battery life, processor speed, and camera technology based on past trends. The next iPhones may also include software innovations, 5G support, and display technology improvements that will improve user experience."

Here's Why 2TB of Storage Is Probably Not Necessary for Your iPhone 15 Pro

A 2TB storage option—eight times the capacity of the entry-level MacBook Air and four times that of the base MacBook Pro—will be available with the upcoming iPhone Pro. However, it's not quite as absurd as it first appears.

The maximum storage capacity of the iPhone 15 Pro is expected to be 2TB, or two thousand gigabytes, based on insider reports. The maximum storage capacity of the current iPhone 14 Pro is 1TB, which is already far too much for most users. Even though there were no new features in the new model, this will be great news for some iPhone owners, making the upgrade worthwhile. Oh, and the iPhone now has USB-C, which is another piece of this puzzle to take into account.

"If iPhone brings USB-C and up to 2TB of storage internal, then if you were on the road and running out of space on your laptop, you could potentially transfer over a bunch of your files to your phone temporarily until you get home to clear things off," Travis Johansen, the filmmaker, said in an email. "A huge benefit of having a two terabyte phone is also just the fact that shooting 360 video in 4k or even 8K takes a ton of space."

'Reckless Abandon' on Record

For high-definition video, there is an evident requirement for additional device capacity. Modern iPhones are powerful film-making devices that can record 4K footage at up to 60 frames per second in Dolby Vision (HDR). It requires a large amount of room. So much space, in fact, if you shoot in Apple's ProRes 4K format, you cannot accomplish it on the smallest 128GB iPhone Pro. To even see the option in the settings, you need to have at least 256GB of storage.

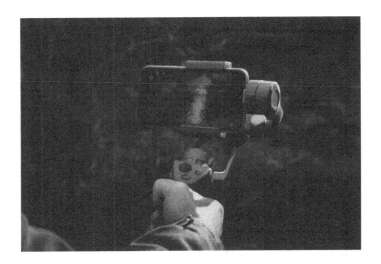

With the advancement of iPhone video capabilities, pros will be able to record TV shows and movies with just a phone. However, storage gets full quickly at that point, and since the iPhone doesn't support external storage (SD cards, for example), you need to make sure you have adequate room.

And it's not just filmmakers. Podcasters, particularly those who use video, and musicians who record numerous audio streams from various participants can also quickly fill up SSDs.

"For me, as a podcaster and content creator, I am definitely interested in the freedom of having that much space to be able to record, edit and store all of the episode assets without being tethered to the cloud," Nate Runkel, a podcaster, said in an email. The fact that I will essentially have a portable podcast studio in my pocket and be able to edit on the fly without worrying about running out of space in the middle of a project appeals to me. Additionally, it will provide me the opportunity to film 4K footage with complete abandon and without fear."

USB-C Boosts Speed of Transfer

But, in contrast to 2021, when Apple increased the storage capacity of the iPhone Pro to 1TB, there will probably be another significant shift in the way we record and store video on our iPhones—USB-C.

As required by the EU, USB-C is set to replace Lightning in the near future. Not only does this eliminate the need for you to carry an additional charging cable specifically for your iPhone, but it also has other benefits.

Lightning moves slowly. It enables USB-C-speed charging, but for data transfer, the iPhone is still limited to USB 2.0 speeds, which are capped at 480 Mbps. Compare that to the 10Gbps maximum that USB-C can support.

This implies that it's nearly hard for a photographer or videographer to get the raw material off your iPhone throughout the workday. Either you need many phones, or you need someone to help you transfer the phones while you continue shooting on a new, empty phone.

And that's before we even talk about the risks associated with not backing up your video as you go. Let's say your phone dies or gets lost and you have a day's worth of video on it.

This might be resolved with USB-C, though it's not a guarantee. The latest iPad Pro model with a Lightning connector was the 2015 edition, which could support USB 3.0 rates of up to 5Gbps. This indicates that Apple had the option to upgrade the Lightning iPhones' transfer speed at any point, but decided against it.

The 2TB iPhone 15 Pro will be a model for the pros in either case. It's true that you could save an infinite number of series, films, pictures, and videos, but why would you? You are able to stream everything. However, this is going to be fantastic news for the pros.

Reasons the iPhone 15 May Not Be the Revolution You're Looking for

It's anticipated that Apple will unveil new gadgets during its next "Wonderlust" event, but you may want to lower your expectations.

It has been reported that Apple is getting ready to release new AirPods with a USB-C charging case in place of the current Lightning port. It has also been stated that the business intends to include USB-C in upcoming iPhone models. The lackluster nature of these improvements may indicate that Apple is reaching a limit in terms of how rapidly and to what extent it can revolutionize rather than iterate its products.

Johan Alexander, CEO of APKCima, said via email that "Apple's commitment to delivering high-quality products and seamless user experiences is unquestionable." But there are certain technological constraints that the tech sector must deal with. It becomes harder to make significant advances in technology, which encourages more iterative design techniques.

Meh, Apple?

There are reports that Apple will unveil a number of goods at its event on September 12. It is reported that all versions will have 35W wireless charging. It looks that the iPhone is one of the first handsets to support the Qi2 standard, which combines wireless and magnetic charging.

The 6.7-inch screen of the suspected iPhone 15 Ultra is

anticipated to have a refresh rate of 120 Hz, thinner bezels, and a new "Action" button that would take the place of the conventional Mute button. This new button, which is a feature of the Apple Watch Ultra, is also expected to be present in the iPhone 15 Pro.

It's unlikely that the Apple Watches of this year—especially the Series 9—will alter all that much. They will probably receive minor speed and battery life improvements, though. New health features might also be implemented. In addition, a fresh shade of pink might be added for the next series.

While useful, USB-C on iPhones and other devices is hardly the stuff of tech fantasies. It is accurate to say that Apple has promised to release the revolutionary Vision Pro headset. But, the headset won't be available until the following year, and at $3500, it will be beyond the budget of many people.

Has Apple lost its magic, then?

Tech expert Arun Dhanaraj wrote in an email, "One possibility is that expectations for Apple's innovation and groundbreaking features have been set so high that anything less might be seen as underwhelming." "Additionally, leaks or speculations about the products may have dampened the element of surprise, leading to a lukewarm response from enthusiasts."

According to Alexander, Apple's need on cutting-edge parts, such as the newest CPUs, to power iPhones, can also cause problems with supply chain availability.

"Balancing the aesthetics and functionality for which Apple is known can sometimes restrict radical design changes," he stated. "Additionally, regulatory constraints can limit innovation in specific areas, such as privacy and security."

Tech expert Mark Vena said in an email that as the smartphone market has grown, it is becoming more challenging to deliver revolutionary innovations with every new edition of the iPhone. "Phone design has reached a point where further enhancements, such as camera improvements or faster processors, can only go so far in driving consumer excitement," he stated. "This limitation is not unique to Apple but affects the entire industry."

Ways Apple Can Continue To Develop

According to Alexander, Apple must make even greater investments in R&D to find or develop novel technologies that have the potential to completely redefine product categories if it is to continue producing innovative products.

"Enhancing the integration between hardware and software is essential to creating more cohesive user experiences," he stated. "Prioritizing sustainability initiatives is becoming increasingly important in addressing environmental concerns."

Vena pointed out that Apple needs to go beyond simply offering incremental hardware updates like connectors or charging standards. He claimed that the corporation may differentiate itself by emphasizing ecosystem integration, user experience improvements, and software breakthroughs.

"Investing in augmented reality (AR), artificial intelligence (AI), and sustainable technologies are areas where Apple can push boundaries," he stated. "Additionally, exploring new product categories or revolutionary form factors could rejuvenate their product lineup."

According to Mac Steer, the creator of the software startup Simify, Apple must likewise innovate its user experience.

"The first time I used an Apple product, it was so intuitive, it felt like I was using something that had been made for me personally," he stated. "It's a shame that they've lost that feeling as they've grown more generic."

9 Uses for the Action Button on the iPhone 15 Pro

The iPhone 15 Pro and Pro Max feature a new button called Action. On earlier iterations as well as the 15 and 15 Plus, it takes the place of the Silent Mode option. You can turn on shortcuts, open programs, and turn off your phone. This is all that you can accomplish.

1 *Start the Silent Mode (Default)*

As with the preceding switch, silent mode is the default setting. Long-press the Action button to use it in its current state. (The button located above the volume controls on the left side of the phone.)

Go to Settings > Action Button and choose an option from the list below to personalize the Action button.

2. *Turn on the camera*

utilize the Action button as a shortcut if you need to utilize the camera more quickly than you can click the app icon. Ideal for taking pictures at a party or when traveling.

3. Select an Accessibility Option

Have a preferred accessibility feature? This button can be used as a shortcut for features like Live Captions, VoiceOver (a screen reader), and color inversion.

4. Record a Voice Note

When conducting fieldwork, research, or any other task requiring you to take quick notes without forgetting anything, having a shortcut to launch a voice memo is invaluable.

5. Start a Quick Cut

Rather than interacting with a Widget or asking Siri, you can use the Action Button to carry out your preferred Shortcut.

For iOS devices, Shortcuts is a free program that you can configure to perform various things, such calculating tips, playing a playlist, finding the travel time to a location without using a navigation tool, and much more.

6. Switch on the torch

Going camping? during a performance held outdoors? Are you having trouble navigating a strange place? With a quick (long) button press, get light. Press it once again to switch it off.

7. Select the Focus Mode

Use the button to turn on and off Focus Mode if you catch yourself daydreaming or fiddling with your phone instead of working on your task. Focus Mode is similar to Do Not Disturb, except it lets you make automatic replies and customize call, message, and notification filters.

8. Open the Magnifier Application

Use the Magnifier app to give yourself a magnifying glass.

9. Interpret a Discussion

This is a terrific idea if you're traveling or interacting with individuals from different languages so you can translate quickly.

CHAPTER 3

Apple Might Stop Making Leather iPhone 15 Cases, Why? This Is Excellent News

It's about time that Apple stopped producing a leather cover for the impending iPhone 15.

Apple is so hot on environmental and ethical problems like privacy, green power, and safeguarding users from uninvited tracking and data theft that it seems weird that the business still sells leather things, especially cases, which are essentially disposables. According to reputable Apple rumor monger DuanRui, Apple will eventually quit using leather to produce iPhone cases—at least for this model. It's past time for Apple to take this action, whether or not the rumor is accurate. The good news is that respectable substitutes are available.

Fashion stylist Nuria Gregori said in an interview, "When I'm choosing clothes for a project and I see non-leather clothing and accessories, I research their sourcing and sustainability." "I don't want to replace leather with something that's not any better."

Look of Leather

Apple has traditionally produced high-quality leather casings. In comparison to their silicone equivalents created by Apple, they are frequently lighter, feel better, last longer, and improve with age. In contrast, the silicone cases can get so grippy that they are difficult to get in and out of a jeans pocket. They also lose chunks out of their corners and become oily if you handle them after using moisturizer.

As leather is essentially a byproduct of the meat industry, purchasing leather goods—like shoes—is not as morally repugnant as purchasing and consuming meat. However, that's not really the issue here.

Apple regularly promotes its environmentally friendly practices, such as using recycled aluminum in its manufacturing process and using only renewable energy for its corporate and retail operations. Being environmentally conscious goes beyond merely addressing the climate problem. It's about being ethically behaved, about sustainability, and about not wasting resources, even when doing so is more difficult or costly.

It's simple to criticize a successful business for not performing well enough. We lament the use of throwaway straws in the artisanal vanilla cola floats at our neighborhood's organic, zero-kilometer ice cream parlor, but we don't mention how much plastic packaging is used for every Amazon order that arrives at our houses. However, this does not imply Apple can get away with things like animal mistreatment, even if it is headed in the right direction.

Furthermore, the manufacture of leather has negative environmental and ethical effects. Leather has a significant environmental impact, ranging from the poisonous chemicals used in the tanning process to the deforestation brought on by the cultivation of animal feed. While it is feasible to lessen the impact and use fewer dangerous chemicals, it is preferable to not participate at all.

Imitating It

For a long time, we have "enjoyed" faux leather goods, such as rough PVC car seats that scorch your exposed skin in the sun and "vegan leather" or leatherette purses, wallets, and upholstery that quickly deteriorate rather than enhancing with age like the genuine thing. Because many substitutes to leather are essentially plastic and manufactured of petroleum-based materials, they might also be questionable from an environmental standpoint.

The fact that there are other choices is excellent news. Fruit leather, such as that from pineapples, mushrooms, grapes, and corks, is derived from plants. These aren't real leather, of course, but they biodegrade fast and are made from vegetable industry byproducts or sustainable, renewable fruit crops, unlike plastic leathers.

It's more difficult to defend the use of leather for a phone cover that will be thrown away when the phone is changed, even though you might have a strong argument for that leather Eames chair and ottoman that will outlive you. Even if these fruit leathers do not wear as well as real leather, it doesn't matter. All they need to do is look attractive and last as long as your phone.

All types of fake leather have improved significantly. Because of the way that leather creases and hangs, fashion manufacturers are even producing very respectable leather clothing, which may be the trickiest to pull off. Furthermore, certain products—like faux sheepskin or the fur collar lining of a denim jacket—have the benefit of being machine washable while still having an almost identical appearance to the genuine thing.""It would be fantastic for the environment and animal welfare if they could find a lovely vegan substitute that is just as good or better," commented iPhone user Parzival in a MacRumors forum discussion.

And Apple, a business renowned for its proficiency with materials, is one of the companies that can create a sustainable substitute for leather. Indeed, Apple leather is currently available, however it may contain as much as 50% plastic.

Why Critics Find the Fine Woven Case of the iPhone 15 So Repulsive

The Verge and numerous other outlets claim that Apple's new $60 FineWoven iPhone cases are awful and instantly display stains and damage. Is this anything else or a FineWovenGate?

People appear to be content with the new iPhone 15. The anticipated consumer outcry over the switch to USB-C appears not to have materialized, while the other odd updates—such as replacing the Action Button with a mute option—have not annoyed anyone. Therefore, it is up to Apple's new FineWoven cases—which do not include a cowskin—to step up and win one for the team. It seems to be the worst case ever created.

Making the move from leather may be viewed as having two consequences. Younes El Kacimi, a tech analyst and journalist, revealed via email that "although it's a step towards sustainability, it seems to have compromised the durability and aesthetic aging that customers loved with the leather cases."

Casegate

The fact that animal skins were being utilized to create items by a corporation as environmentally conscious as Apple always seemed a little strange, but that is no longer the case. Apple's now-discontinued leather cases have been replaced with FineWoven casings. The majority of their material is post-consumer recycled "content," most likely polyester or other plastic. The case's sides are made of a somewhat more durable material than the rear, which is covered with an extremely finely woven twill-like fabric.

Because it replaces Apple's leather cases and because it costs $59, the FineWoven case comes with some expectations. The best aspect of leather is that it gets better as it matures. Over time, abrasions, scratches, rubs, and nicks all disappear, giving the case personality. We could anticipate that its successor will act similarly. The FineWoven's availability in significantly dimmer hues is its lone benefit above the $59 silicone case.

"Received and given back. Owner of a FineWoven case for a brief period of time, teeshot4, comments, "Felt cheap almost like cardboard," in a MacRumors forum discussion.

However, the FineWoven doesn't seem to age like animal tanned skin. The FineWoven wallet case that writer Allison Johnson of The Verge received for evaluation already had some wear on the corners. Furthermore, Nilay Patel, the top editor of The Verge, constantly scraped his fingers over a FineWoven case, producing scratch marks that are likely to last a lifetime.

An Argument in Favor of Apple

Is this really so horrible, though? Scratches are common in cases, and even leather, which can absorb damage and develop an eye-catching patina, can still have dings and scratches. It's not as though they vanish.

Arthur Shi of iFixit took a FineWoven case and examined it using a strong digital microscope. Shi discovered that the threads are only 1/12 the width of a human hair, or 6 microns thick. That black line running between the threads in this picture is a hair.

They discovered that even a severe scratch won't break the threads in the twill weave, which is incredibly resistant to tearing and abrasion. However, the scratch will permanently alter the weave, giving the appearance of being scratched.

Naturally, we will have to wait and watch how these cases develop. FineWoven's fabric is likely to absorb finger grease and other common dirt, much like leather, and then boldly display those stains as eye-catching patterns. Or perhaps more akin to denim, a material that seems to get better with wear.

And to be honest, who else but a prosumer would try to ruin or even break their $59 buy by dragging their nails across it? Customers will treat their cases with considerably more care, and the cases may wear exquisitely. Not quite like jeans, not quite like leather, but gorgeous all the same. Additionally, Apple has a track record of success with cases. Although they are never inexpensive, they are always durable, light, and sturdy. I purchased Apple's Smart Folio case for the 12.9-inch iPad Pro in 2018, and even though it started to show signs of wear this year, I still use it.

Like all the other iconic Apple gates, I think Casegate will eventually become little more than a gimmick used by tech news websites to generate a little bit of user interaction out of thin air.

A Roundup of 2024's Top iPhone 15 Cases

Because of their protruding multi-lens camera arrays and full-glass back panels, Apple's iPhones are both costly to purchase and repair. It is wise to invest in a case to safeguard it.

We picked out a few of our favorite cases from among the many available, which range from sleek covers to robust protectors to folding wallets.

The ESR MagSafe Silicone Cover and Stand, the Best Option for the iPhone 15 Pro in Every Way

Pros:

- Protection against scratches and impact

- Stand conveniently integrated

- Compatible with MagSafe

Downside:

- Not many color choices

Made of soft, scratch-resistant silicone, the ESR Cloud Soft Case is compatible with MagSafe and has an adjustable stand so you can watch videos, read, or use your phone without holding it. Carrying your phone is also an option. The ability to charge your iPhone simultaneously is available while using it in landscape mode.

This iPhone case is fashionable, durable, and easy to carry anywhere.

Supremely Clear CaseThe Spigen MagFit Elite Hybrid Magnetic Case for the iPhone 15

Pros:

- Protect your iPhone with a transparent case.

- Compatible with MagSafe

Drawbacks:

- Expensive.

Protect your iPhone from drops and scratches with Spigen's Magnetic Ultra Hybrid MagFit case. This clear plastic case lets you show off your phone. Protecting the screen and cameras from harm, it features raised edges and Air Cushion Technology, which is military grade.

In order to keep your iPhone safe without drawing attention to itself, this case is a great pick.

I love using my card holder. Magnetic Wallet Card Holder by Spigen Smart Fold (MagFit) Benefits:

Pros:

- Functions as a stand

- Protects two cards at once

Drawback:

- Expensive

Elegant and functional, the Spigen Smart Fold (MagFit) Magnetic Wallet Card Holder features two card slots and a clever foldable stand for convenient hands-free use. To top it all off, it retains its pocket-friendly compact profile.

The practicality and aesthetics of this case are perfectly balanced.

Would You Prefer These Instead?

- My phone is an iPhone 14. Protect your iPhone from harm with the OtterBox Defender. Its synthetic rubber exterior and strong Polycarbonate (PC) interior will keep your device safe from harm.

- I own a 13-inch iPhone. A sturdy case with an integrated cardholder, the Incipio Stashback is both stylish and practical. Up to three credit/ID cards or banknotes can be securely carried without sacrificing the sleek design.

- For my case, I'm looking for something exceptional. The handcrafted Blood Eyeball case by Techypop is sure to turn heads. Screaming inconveniently!

Measurements That Matter When Choosing an iPhone Case.

Size: Although there is a range of sizes available for Apple's phones, upgrading may not necessitate a new cover. But you'll have to get a new case if you go from an iPhone to an iPhone Pro or vice versa. Some cases are made to fit a certain model, while others are compatible with several. So, be sure to check the compatibility before you purchase a case.

Fit. A slender phone can become an awkward piece of technology with the addition of some cases, which increase its weight and size significantly.

Protection. Some cases are only cosmetic, while others will practically protect your phone from harm. The trade-off for toughness is usually a larger phone. A screen protector, which comes as an extra accessory with many phone covers, is another crucial factor to think about.

Picks for the Finest OtterBox iPhone Covers

The OtterBox Defender is the best phone cover we've ever used, and we think everyone should get one.

What Makes Us Reliable?

For my job as a tech reporter, I've tested out a wide variety of iPhone covers and pouches. As someone who frequently drops their phone, I can attest to the significance of protective cases and the abuse they endure.

If you own an iPhone15,14, or 13—and use MagSafe—then you need this Otterbox Defender Series XT.

In brief: Protect your smartphone to an unprecedented degree with the OtterBox Defender Series XT for MagSafe. Its multi-layer construction ensures a snug fit.

Pros:

- Extremely shielding

- Affordably sized

- A snug fit for your phone

Downside:

- Rightfully large

- Not designed to work with other brands of camera cases

Feel completely protected with an OtterBox Defender XT for MagSafe cover for your iPhone 15, 14, or 13. You can rest assured that your phone will stay put thanks to the case's front frame, which also features an elevated ridge for added drop protection. For convenient wireless charging, it is also MagSafe-compatible.

This phone case, according to OtterBox, can withstand

drops equal to or greater than the military standard. To protect the screen and camera from breaking, it has raised edges.

We were pleasantly surprised by how simple it was to put the cover on, because assembling multi-layer phone cases with separate front and back sections is usually a real pain. Despite the fact that it needs some assembly, getting on took no more than a minute.

Despite its durability, this phone case was surprisingly lightweight. I bought it because of the design and how it made me feel.

You can also get the OtterBox Defender Series XT for MagSafe for the following iPhone models: 15 Plus, 15 Pro, and 15 Pro Max.

Super Cheap OtterBox Commuter Series for MagSafe (iPhone 15, iPhone 14, and iPhone 13)

In brief: For those on a budget, OtterBox has you covered with their Commuter Series for MagSafe. Putting on and locking in the two-layer case is a breeze.

Pros:

- Offers a double layer of defense

- Less expensive than competing OtterBox cases

- Simple assembly

Downside:

- The Defender Series offers better drop protection.

Comparable to the Defender in appearance, but in reverse, is the Commuter's casing design. An inner layer of synthetic rubber snaps into a protective plastic casing. You may still acquire a good hold on the phone because some synthetic rubber is still visible on the sides. You can use this cover with your iPhone15,14, or 13.

When compared to the military standard, this case offers three times the protection against drops. While it may not offer the same level of protection as the OtterBox Defender Series case, most consumers will find it sufficient.

If you're on a tighter budget, but still want top-notch protection, this case is a great alternative to the Defender OtterBox.

Along with the iPhone 15 Plus, 15 Pro, and 15 Pro Max, the OtterBox Commuter Series for MagSafe is compatible with the following models:

Elegant ChoiceProtect your iPhone15,14, or 13 with OtterBox's Symmetry Series Clear for MagSafe.

In brief: With a wide array of colors and styles to choose from, the OtterBox Symmetry Series Clear for MagSafe is the perfect phone case for style-conscious consumers looking for protection.

Pros:

- Minimalist style

- Various types and hues

- Compatible with MagSafe

Downside:

- It isn't as sturdy as other OtterBox cases.

The OtterBox Symmetry is the most beautiful and sophisticated option for a phone case that offers excellent protection from drops. It's sturdy without looking as bulky as the Defender or Commuter models. Also, no other scenario that we suggest is as comprehensive as the Symmetry. It's not possible to put it all together.

Both the Commuter and the Defender were compatible with the wireless and MagSafe chargers I own. Only the Symmetry had excellent locking with the MagSafe charger. For that reason, it's a great option for you if you like that style.

The case's raised edge provides exceptional protection for the phone's rear camera. It is unnecessary to protrude the camera protection ridge to provide equal support in the Defender and Commuter cases due to their thicker construction. Because of the elongated camera ridge, the Symmetry cover sits at an angle, elevating the top of the phone.

- Is anyone else a fan of it? As far as iPhone cases go, Rolling Stone says the OtterBox Symmetry is the greatest all-around option.

- Who are the purchasers? Protective, well-fitting, and simple to install, this case has received rave reviews from customers on Amazon. Nearly eighty-one percent of the more than 2,800 customers who reviewed the iPhone 13 on Amazon were satisfied with their purchase.

You can also get the OtterBox Symmetry Series Clear for MagSafe for the following iPhone models: 15 Plus, 15 Pro, and 15 Pro Max.

Would You Prefer These Instead?

- A more refined style would be ideal for me. An upscale option for quality leather cases is the OtterBox Strada Folio Series.

- A firmer grasp on my phone would be great. To improve your grip or use it as a stand for your phone, the OtterBox OtterGrip Symmetry series comes with replaceable PopGrips.

Tips for Detecting

Things to keep in mind when looking for an OtterBox protection for your phone are:

- Drop testing is a must for every OtterBox case to

guarantee it will keep your device safe.

- You should look for an OtterBox that has a snug fit for your smartphone.

- Consideration of Design: A well-designed phone case should both protect your device and complement your personal style.

- Guarantee that you will receive a new case in the event that the one you receive is damaged or does not work properly with a solid guarantee that demonstrates the brand's confidence in its goods.

- Antimicrobial Characteristics (Preferential): If you want to keep your phone clean and germ-free, consider obtaining an antimicrobial or easily-cleanable case.

Protection

Look for a phone that has a raised bezel around the screen and rear camera(s) and a protective casing for the greatest protection. When you drop your phone, these raised edges will keep it from breaking. To ensure they can withstand heavy drops without harming your phone, OtterBox puts every one of their phone cases through rigorous testing.

Fit

The greatest way to keep your phone safe is to use a case that fits snugly. Because of how snugly they fit, many people like the multi-layer or multi-piece OtterBox cases. When shopping for an OtterBox case, make sure you choose the one that fits your device correctly. OtterBox produces protection for the vast majority of Android and Apple mobile devices.

Design

When looking for an OtterBox case, keep your personal style in mind. A wider variety of colors is available for certain models, including the OtterBox Symmetry.

Additionally, the various OtterBox models vary in terms of weight. When it comes to protecting their phones, some individuals prefer bulkier cases. If you're looking for more protection for your phone, OtterBox has a few variants with multiple layers. On the other hand, some people favor minimalist designs with only one layer of protection, such as the OtterBox Symmetry.

Protection Plan

The warranty is an important factor to think about when purchasing a phone case. If the case breaks within the guarantee period, the manufacturer will replace it, demonstrating their commitment to their product. The smartphone cases made by OtterBox come with a Limited Lifetime Warranty. The "Lifetime of the product," as defined by OtterBox, is seven years from the date of purchase. This guarantee covers that period.

Optional Antimicrobial Characteristics

Because of all the handling and dropping your phone case does, it becomes readily infected with bacteria. You can clean any OtterBox case with ease. If you value cleanliness above all else, though, you might want to look into purchasing the OtterBox phone cases that are antimicrobial. In order to prevent the growth of microbes, the antimicrobial versions use silver additions.

FAQ

If I have an OtterBox Defender case, how can I open it?

There are three parts to the OtterBox Defender Case: the holster, the rubber cover, and the hard shell. You can remove each layer. The plastic holster is the top layer; to remove it, unclip the four corners individually. The next step is to remove the plastic housing from the rubber cover. If you're having trouble getting under the cover, try removing the little rubber tab from the device and unscrewing the flap that covers the charging port. Then you'll have no trouble sliding your finger under any of the edges. You can now remove the case's frame from the back by releasing the clips located on the bottom of the intact plastic case. You can find these clips on the phone's edges, as well as its top and bottom. You can remove the back cover and frame from the phone by releasing the clips.

Is wireless charging compatible with OtterBox cases?

Although the effectiveness of wireless charging may differ between charger types and certain handsets, all OtterBox smartphone covers are compatible with this technology.

Qi and MagSafe are the two most popular wireless charging protocols currently available. The MagSafe chargers are designed to quickly charge iPhones 12 and later, but you can use either one to charge any wirelessly charged phone. Even while you can charge your MagSafe phone through the case, you won't get the full benefit of the faster MagSafe rates if the OtterBox case doesn't have the special MagSafe magnets. For optimal MagSafe functioning, be sure to have an OtterBox case that says "with MagSafe."

Do OtterBox cases provide water resistance?

While certain OtterBox cases may be waterproof, the majority of those with the DROP+ rating are only water-resistant. Without the DROP+ protection grade, a case is not water-resistant. They are water-resistant, so they won't be damaged if they are splashed. Keep your phone out of water unless it's waterproof; OtterBox doesn't promise their cases will keep it safe while immersed.

CHAPTER 4

One of the most anticipated updates to the iPhone in a long time is the action button.

Despite how ridiculous it sounds, the Action button alone may make the new iPhone 15 Pro more desirable than the base model.

Apple has introduced a new customisable Action button in the iPhone 15 Pro, which has supplanted the long-standing silent toggle switch. From starting the camera app to activating voice memos or performing user-customizable shortcuts, this button can do pretty much anything. Amazingly, it makes your iPhone function as a field recorder, camera, and flashlight—all while being incredibly accessible.

Having an Action button on your toolbar is a good idea. I still believe the vast majority of users will only use it as a camera, despite its extensive customization options. Because capturing anything is currently such a bother, you frequently lose out on precious moments with your children, pets, amusing life stuff, etc., and that is the largest pain point it fixes. Salient PR's founder and CEO, Justin Mauldin, revealed the news in an email.

Silent Location

Even on the iPad, the original mute button was present until Apple got rid of it. It's been there from the start of the iPhone. There was some personalization options for the iPad version as well. It has other potential uses, such as muting alert and notification sounds or locking the screen so it doesn't automatically rotate when you lay down to read.

So, there is a button that can be customized, but the Action button is completely unique and has far more customization options. To begin with, rather of a sliding switch with two separate locations, there is now a real button you may push. As before, it prevents inadvertent activation by muzzling your iPhone with a lengthy press; nonetheless, it falls short when compared to the original switch in this regard.

Unlike with a push button, you can feel or peek at the sliding mute switch to find its position. To let you know how things are doing, the iPhone displays an animation on the new Dynamic Island and makes a unique haptic blip; but, you can't access this information without pressing the button (which also turns off mute).

Some people may find this annoying if they use their phones frequently to mute and unmute, but the Action button has so many other uses that it's worth it. What if you always keep your phone on silent? A new button with no compromises has just been added to your arsenal.

Points of Engagement

You may assign anything to the new button, which is obviously modeled after the Apple Watch Ultra's Action button. There are a lot of built-in options on an iPhone, such as the camera, voice memo, flashlight, magnifier, Do Not Disturb, accessibility settings, and yes, mute.

The majority of users will probably have the camera app open when they press the Action button. Or, with Shortcuts, customers can make it work just like the built-in camera app by launching their preferred third-party software. We won't know for sure until the launch, but I would be surprised if the button didn't also take a picture in this scenario.

"This ought to roll out by default. According to Henrikhelmers, an Apple devotee and iPhone user, "I bet they will make it the default after everyone is used to control silent mode with software." This commentary was made in a MacRumors forum discussion.

This little upgrade brings the iPhone closer to specialized hardware for certain jobs, which will greatly benefit anyone using it. For instance, the iPhone has surpassed specialized pocket recorders as the go-to device for making short audio recordings, whether they be of yourself taking notes or of the environment to use in music production.

Every time you need to use one of those gadgets, you have to turn it on. That means you have to wait for it to boot up even when the sound or idea you were going to record is fading away. Teenage Engineering's TP-7 Digital Tape Recorder, which retails for $1,500, is the only hardware recorder that I am aware of that has an instant-memo feature. Now, with specialized audio apps, the iPhone 15 Pro can accomplish the same—and it's still more affordable!

In terms of accessibility, the Action button is crucial as well. For example, the magnifier is one of the default action choices. It transforms the iPhone's camera into a zoomable magnifier, making it easier for older eyes to read any printed menus that may still be there.

While the new camera functions and titanium-coated band of the iPhone 15 Pro may be more thrilling, the Action button is likely to have a larger impact on people's daily lives than any other hardware feature introduced by Apple this year.

Reasons Why the New iPhone 15 Pro Could Eliminate Physical Control Buttons

Virtual haptic switches could replace all physical buttons

on the next iPhone, allowing users to adjust the volume and power without touching the screen.

Even if Joni Ive's departure from Apple may have given you the impression that the War on Buttons had finished, it appears to be dragging on. Analyst Ming-Chi Kuo claims that the iPhone 15 might replace the actual power and volume buttons with touch controls that provide haptic feedback. While this may increase the iPhone's durability, it also has the potential to significantly increase its annoyance level.

The company made the right call when it decided to replace the traditional home button with a haptic engine; the results speak for themselves. "The haptic button eliminated the problem of mechanical home buttons, which used to happen all the time," said technology journalist Ahmed N.Khan via email.

Taptic Feeling

Apple is no stranger to this. If you exclude keyboards, the total number of virtual buttons on its products can be more than the number of physical mechanical buttons. Apple introduced the Force Touch trackpad in 2015 to replace the mechanical trackpad button on MacBooks. It was simply a silvered-out touchscreen similar to the iPhone. These trackpads were completely mechanical. A tiny vibration mechanism that Apple has subsequently included into numerous gadgets, dubbed a Taptic Engine, was responsible for the click.

The Taptic Engine's haptic feedback is so lifelike that it's hard to tell it wasn't a button click. Try holding down the virtual home button when the phone is turned off if you're using an older iPhone model (such as a 7 or 8). Oh no, it already died. Complete inaction.

Since then, Apple has integrated virtual buttons into a number of its products. The Digital Crown on the Apple Watch, the squeeze-shaft button on the AirPods Pro, and similar devices. In addition to vibration warnings and tactile keyboard feedback, the Taptic Engine enhances the iPhone experience.

Simplified with No Buttons

A virtual button that clicks using a Taptic mechanism has the advantage of being long-lasting. Prior to the Force Touch version, I had problems with the majority of the trackpads on my MacBooks. A virtual button eliminates the possibility of broken mechanisms. Even if that's not the case, it might be feasible to reposition those buttons so that they're more ergonomically sound.

Press and hold the AirPods Pro 2's volume button. These pick up on a brief up or down swipe and respond by adjusting the volume by a single click. Picture this: while viewing a video in landscape mode on your iPhone, you could swipe anywhere on either side, or even the top and bottom corners. I think that would be really cool.

On the other hand, there are drawbacks. A virtual switch's inability to detect when you push a button is the most significant drawback. For example, to access a dedicated setup menu when starting up a MacBook, you can hardwire its power/TouchID button.

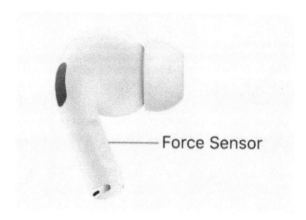

Force Sensor

In order to accommodate the iPhone 7's solid-state virtual home button, Apple rearranged the device's emergency controls. There was a time when you could press and hold the home button and the sleep/wake buttons to initiate a reset in the event that your device locked up. The iPhone 7 made that process obsolete, replacing it with a combination of the volume down and sleep/wake keys.

Restarting an iOS 16 phone is more akin to inputting a cheat code on a vintage SEGA or Nintendo system. The steps are as follows: push and release the volume up button, then the volume down button. Then, while holding the side button, release it when you see the Apple logo, according to Apple's help website.

Think about how the dance would change if you could no longer press any buttons.

Furthermore, important spatial signals will be lost if Apple adopts swipe controllers for volume control. The volume buttons are clearly marked and easy to reach. For use when the light is off, you may also use them to steady your iPhone. Both usability and accessibility depend on this.

It will be intriguing to observe Apple's resolution to these issues. It would be great if it's another impressive solution, like the Dynamic Island, and not another useless one, like the Touch Bar that was on the MacBooks but is now dead.

Reasons Why Charging Your iPhone Over 80% Is Nearly Never Necessary

By avoiding a full charge, the iPhone 15 can extend the life of your battery.

The new iPhone 15's Settings app's Battery section now includes more detailed battery information. An additional function that can be enabled to extend the life of the battery is the ability to cap the maximum charge to 80% of its complete capacity.

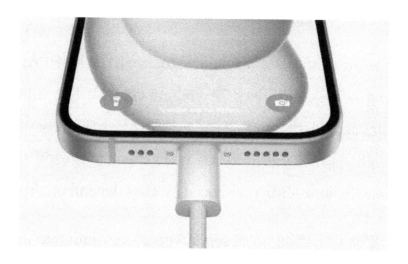

One thing you can do to make your phone's battery last longer is to charge it no more than 80% of the capacity. Most smartphones use lithium-ion batteries, which naturally degrade with time but are hastened by heat and repeated full charge cycles. James Herman, founder of MobileTech Addicts, revealed via email that reducing the amount of charging to 80 percent will help your battery survive longer by reducing the amount of heat and stress.

Status of the Battery: Catch 22

This is perplexing. You should only charge your battery to 80 percent capacity if you want it to survive as long as feasible before replacement. Say you typically get about ten hours off of a single charge for your phone. Eight hours is the maximum time you can get out of a fully charged battery.

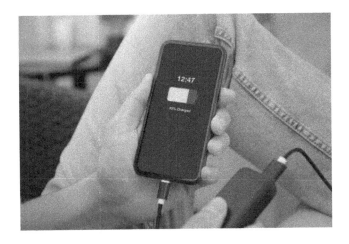

Reducing the amount of time you charge your battery defeats the purpose of maintaining its health if extending the time between charges is your primary goal. Then what's your next move? Saving your phone's maximum battery capacity is pointless if you never plan on using it.

To get through the day, the majority of users should leave the default settings and fully utilize their battery capacity. "A slightly slower degrading battery is preferable than running out of charge," remarks Kim. "What really degrades lithium batteries faster (apart from consumption) is extreme temperature and time spent at a high or low state of charge."

Ultimately, it's up to you and how you utilize your phone. This configuration is ideal if you never leave the house or if you have a convenient way to charge your phone at work. However, if you are constantly on the go and rely on a backup battery to get you through the day, you might as well charge your phone to full capacity every time.

Reasonable Steps

Phone batteries despise being totally full or empty, and they are damaged when charged to more than 80% while hot, so it's smart to limit how much power you use them. For this reason, rapid chargers flood a battery with juice up to 80% capacity before reducing the flow to a trickle for the last 20%.

When compared to slow charging, rapid charging causes the battery to overheat. Having a quick charger on your bedside is unnecessary. Michael Kim, creator and editor of EV Charger Review and a battery expert, revealed via email that he uses a standard 5V USB charger. Optimized Battery Charging is already built into the iPhone; it remembers how you usually charge it and keeps the battery at 80% overnight so it can charge to 100% just before you need it. Already, this shortens the amount of time the battery needs to be fully charged.

You may still create a Shortcut that notifies you when the battery reaches 80% so you can manually remove it from the charger, even if you don't own an iPhone 15.

However, you may extend the life of your battery in various ways.

"You can also prolong the battery life on your iPhone by dimming the screen slightly, shortening the time until sleep mode kicks in, using power-saver mode, limiting notifications and location services, and locking your phone when not in use," revealed Steven Athwal, a consumer electronics retailer and telecoms expert based in the UK, in an email.

Every time you use your phone, there's a tradeoff compared to when you don't. You can save battery life by disabling a lot of functions, but eventually, it becomes useless to have a phone in the first place.

Use the iPhone's default settings (since Apple understands better than anyone how to charge its battery), avoid charging in direct sunlight, never charge in a hot environment, and make smart decisions to save power. Is it necessary to have your screen turned on constantly, or is it possible to have it switch off after a certain amount of time?

However, it's a futile effort in the end. Dyeing will occur in the battery. The iPhone 15 makes it much easier to replace, though.

The Critical Need for Rapid USB Data Transfer on the iPhone Pro

Possibly, the iPhone 15 Pro will get USB 3.0 transfer rates at last. All iPhones, including the Pro, continue to use the older USB 2.0 standard.

The video capabilities of Apple's flagship iPhones are much lauded, and rightfully so. These phones can record stunning 4K footage at high frame rates. But you'll need to use a USB 2.0 legacy connection if you wish to move the footage to an iPad, Mac, or PC for editing purposes. The supply-chain expert Ming-Chi Kuo claims that this will be resolved in the iPhone Pro that is released in the following year. The worst part? There will be no changes to the standard iPhone 15.

"The iPhone Pro is a powerhouse of a phone, but its lack

of USB 3.0 port means transferring videos and photos off the device can be painfully slow," revealed Jeroen van Gils, managing director at networking tech startup Lifi.co, via email.

Delays in Adoption

With ProRes, the iPhone can capture 4K video at 30 frames per second. View the following in your phone's camera settings: "A minute of 10-bit HDR ProRes is approximately 1.7GB for HD and 6GB for 4K."

Six gigabytes of space for a thirty-second film. Now we can test how quickly the data can be transferred from the phone using USB. USB 2.0 has a maximum data transfer rate of 480 Mbps, which is, if I'm not mistaken, only 60 MB/s. Ideally, the transfer would take more than a minute and a half; however, everyone who has attempted to transfer large files over USB 2.0 knows that it would take much longer. Quite a while, in fact, to warrant brewing some coffee.

The maximum data transfer rate for USB 3 (the most recent version) is 10 Gbps, or 1.25 GB/s. Here, you wouldn't have time to even consider making that coffee because your minute of 4K ProRes video would be finished before you could.

Because the iPhone Pro now only has a USB 2.0 port, moving big video files might be a real drag. This becomes much more problematic when you think about how big video files can get on an iPhone Pro," tech writer James Calderon said in an email. The data transfer rate of USB 3.0 is up to ten times faster than that of USB 2.0. That implies it would be much quicker to transfer a video file from the iPhone Pro.

That is to say, when it comes to data transfer methods in

the year 2022, USB 2 is pitiful. It's still adequate for charging low-power devices and connecting music devices (very low data speeds needed), but that's about it.

USB-C with AirDrop

Thus, the transition to USB 3 will likely occur for the iPhone 15 Pro at the same time as the EU-mandated change from a Lighting to a USB-C connector. Also likely to undergo the change is the simple iPhone 15, however given the current state of affairs, Apple may manage to cram in yet another generation of Lightning iPhones.

Does a plain old iPhone really require USB 3 anyway?

Perhaps not. After all, how often do you hear iPhone users complaining about the slow transfer speed? Charging and hooking up connected headphones or speakers are the most common uses for cables.

With AirDrop, an iPhone user may establish a direct Wi-Fi connection with another iPhone, making the transfer of large data quick and easy. Because it uses a peer-to-peer connection instead than relying on an existing Wi-Fi network, it stays fast even when you're in the middle of nowhere, like in the woods.

Because AirDrop speeds are dependent on so many outside variables, Apple chooses not to disclose them. It will be far faster than, say, attempting to transfer media to an iPhone 6 from a sports hall crowded with operating microwave ovens, provided that both devices are close and have the most recent versions of Wi-Fi.

From my experience, I can say that AirDrop is faster than USB 2.0 and much more convenient than other options. It's as easy as sending a file from the regular share sheet, and the receivers are always prepared to receive it.

In short, yes, a faster wired connection is required for consistent, dependable file uploads when using the iPhone Pro as a professional-level video camera. But what about the rest of us? As is, it appears to be alright.

Methods for Making Use of Satellite-Based Roadside Assistance

If you own an iPhone, you may learn how to use the

Roadside Assistance via Satellite feature in this article. To use this function, you'll need an iOS 17 device, which means an iPhone14, iPhone 14 Pro, iPhone 15, or iPhone 15 Pro. It differs from other iPhone SOS capabilities, but functions similarly to Emergency SOS via Satellite.

Simple Steps to Use Your iPhone to Call for Satellite Assistance When You Need It

Even though it's only available in extreme cases, both the iPhone 14 and the iPhone 15 are capable of connecting to a satellite. Even while you won't be able to make calls or send normal texts via satellite, it's an option in case you get stuck somewhere without Wi-Fi or cellular connection.

You can reach AAA through Roadside Assistance by Satellite if you ever find yourself in a similar situation, such as being locked out of your car, running out of gas, having a flat tire, or requiring a tow. You can reach out to emergency services through Emergency SOS via satellite in the event of an accident or other life-threatening crisis.

How to use the feature that provides roadside assistance by satellite:

- Press the New Message button in Messages after opening the app.

- Fill out the address field with Roadside.

- Select Roadside Assistance through Satellite.

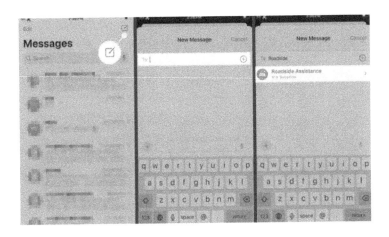

Please be aware that this option will only be displayed if you are in a location without cellphone service or Wi-Fi.

- For each issue, tap the option that best describes it.

- To set up a satellite connection, just follow the on-screen instructions.

Keep in mind that in order to make and keep a connection, you'll have to move your phone around while holding it. If you need to move or make a left or right turn, you can follow the on-screen suggestions for that.

- A AAA agent will be able to assist you once the connection is made. You can respond to the AAA agent's questions regarding your whereabouts and current condition by sending them a text message.

- To keep the satellite connection active until help arrives, keep following the on-screen instructions.

Keep your phone out and follow the on-screen prompts to reestablish the connection if it is interrupted.

How Does Satellite-Based Roadside Assistance Work?

The iPhone 15 and 14 both have a safety feature called Roadside Assistance by Satellite that makes advantage of emergency satellite connectivity. This feature is only accessible on phones that have been upgraded to iOS 17 or later, or on phones that have the necessary hardware to make a satellite connection; it is not available on phones that do not have these features.

Access AAA, a roadside help provider, by satellite with this function. Whenever you use this service, a representative from AAA will ask you to describe your issue and where you are. Among the many roadside emergencies they may help with include low petrol, car locks, and flat tires. Usually, a nearby AAA tow truck or light service car will be dispatched to help you out.

A lot like Apple's Emergency SOS via Satellite, Roadside Assistance via Satellite can get you out of a jam. Unlike other iPhone SOS capabilities, this one doesn't require any prior setup or preparation on your part beyond making sure your phone is up-to-date. When you're in an area without cellular coverage and your iPhone is 14 or 15 and running iOS 17 or later, you can utilize this feature to fix your car.

Where Can I Find Satellite-Based Roadside Assistance?

Only users in the US (including all 50 states and PR) can access this service. Additionally, the feature is only usable in areas without cellular coverage, as it activates only when you try to message roadside assistance without a cellular connection. The standard methods of contacting roadside help can be used by any phone that can establish a connection to a cell tower or a Wi-Fi network.

Is There a Fee for Satellite-Based Roadside Assistance?

For two years following activation, the Roadside Assistance by Satellite feature is complimentary on the iPhone 14 and iPhone 15. After that time ends, Apple has the option to either charge for the function or extend the free period.

There are several linked AAA services that cost money, even if the Roadside Assistance via Satellite feature itself is free. You can use this tool without being a AAA member, however there will usually be a fee for the services provided. Prior to the dispatch of a tow truck or service vehicle to your location, the AAA agent will apprise you of any potential charges. The services you're looking for might already be part of your AAA membership package.

A Periscope Lens for the iPhone Could Revolutionize Everything

A potentially game-changing upgrade to the camera system could be available in the iPhone 15 with a brand new lens design.

Rumor has claimed that the iPhone 15 from 2023 will include a periscope lens, which might allow for an optical zoom range of up to 10x. That would open up a world of possibilities for Apple's computational photography tricks and gimmicks, including improved background blur, incredible close-up images of far-away subjects, and much more.

"While many Android flagships, like Samsung's Galaxy S21 Ultra, have already featured telephoto lenses for a long time, the iPhone 15 series is slated to go official in 2023, which will give [Apple] enough time to tweak its periscope lenses [for] amazing photo quality," Victoria Mendoza, who explains technology, wrote.

Live Periscope

The name of this type of lens says it all: a periscope. To circumvent the most significant optical limitation of smartphone cameras—the focal length—this lens employs a mirror (or prism) to reflect light at an angle of 90 degrees.

A lens requires additional glass (or plastic) components to provide high-magnification telephoto or zoom. A smartphone just does not have the room necessary for this. Increasingly large camera humps have been the response thus far, but this won't solve the problem forever. The solution is to position the lens such that it lies flat within the camera, rather than protruding. This lens is simply reflected light from the periscope.

With all that extra room, Apple might upgrade the camera's optical zoom from 3x to a genuine 10x, replacing the 3x on the iPhone 13 Pro. The next time you want to capture a photo of that strange-looking bird perched in the tree outside your flat, you could be more successful this time.

Close the View

A 10x telephoto lens is most commonly used to get closer shots of distant objects. A 10x zoom is the same as 24mm-240mm on 35mm film cameras or full-frame digital SLRs.

A 240mm 10x pericope lens has been there for a while; it's also on the 2020 Huawei P40 Pro Plus. However, the lens's inherent magnification is just half the tale. When Apple integrates their remarkable computational photography abilities with this 10x range, what kinds of things could it do?

In my opinion, Apple is severely lacking in the telephoto lens department. On the MacRumors forum, iPhone user AirunJae opines, "I like finally having a little more reach with the 3x, but the quality of photos isn't all that great unless there's a lot of light, and even then sometimes it's not as good as I think it should be."

However, not all long zooms are beneficial. Aside from their massive size, which the periscope manages to conceal, they possess two major drawbacks. You can see every tremor in your hand magnified. Second, compared to a wider lens of the same size, they usually let less light in.

Apple's night mode does remarkable job in low light, and the company might use data from the other, more sensitive, cameras to generate a hybrid picture.

The way to fix the shaking has also been established. To compensate for hand movements, shake reduction is a feature of many contemporary cameras. This is achieved by adjusting the lens or the sensor. One feature that will likely be available in the iPhone 15 is sensor-shift shake reduction, which was recently added to the iPhone by Apple. It is much easier to move sensors quickly enough than glass lenses, particularly 10x zoom lenses, because sensors are smaller and lighter.

What is the benefit of an iPhone?

If you already have a long, optically stabilized telephoto lens, why not make it even more useful by adding some technological wizardry? Portrait Mode, one of Apple's most innovative features, mimics the effect of a larger camera's blurred background. The Portrait Mode algorithms could benefit from more precise depth data, because a telephoto lens inevitably produces more blur on the background.

One of the continuing benefits of cameras over phones is the greater variety of lenses available. Is the new periscope lens so good that you can get rid of your bulky camera?

Wait a minute.

In some respects, purpose-built cameras are still superior to phone cameras. One advantage is that they can capture more light thanks to their larger telephoto lenses. The fact that you can change the lenses to achieve a very broad or very long view is another perk. In addition, the background blur is realistic, which is still far better than simulations. Plus, the larger size of their sensors allows them to capture more light and provide a higher level of detail.

Last but not least, it's more convenient and enjoyable to use a camera that has a viewfinder, buttons, knobs, and dials.

However, a genuine 10x optical zoom will significantly improve the quality of most people's images. What does Apple do with it? I'm really curious.

Acknowledgments

The Glory of this book success goes to God Almighty and my beautiful Family, Fans, Readers & well-wishers, Customers and Friends for their endless support and encouragements.

Author Profile

Meet Chris Amber, the energetic writer behind "EnergyCyclist Publishing" who specializes in technology and gadget books. His love of dissecting the intricacies of modern technology has made him a respected authority in the area.

Background: Chris was eager to learn about the complex world of technology when he first started his adventure into it. Equipped with a technical studies degree, he immersed himself in the rapidly changing field of innovation, aiming to provide both enthusiasts and inquisitive minds with an understanding of the newest devices and technological breakthroughs.

Expertise: Chris has a deep understanding of the rapidly changing technology sector and focuses on producing incisive and easily understood material that helps users understand complicated technological ideas. His skill is not just in breaking down the technical nuances but also in turning them into captivating stories that appeal to a wide range of people.

Enthusiasm for Gadgets: Chris's passion for gadgets comes through in everything he writes. He enthusiastically navigates the fast-paced world of innovation, covering everything from wearables to smartphones to cutting-edge tech trends, making sure his readers stay educated and empowered in an era of rapid technological progress.

Highlights of Publications: Chris Amber is the author of several critically acclaimed books that explore various facets of technology and gadgets. His books are guides that lead readers on a thrilling voyage through the intriguing nexus of human life and technical growth, not just manuals.

Philosophy: Chris Amber is an advocate for universal access to technology. His writing style is centered on dissecting difficult ideas into manageable chunks so that his audience feels empowered and understood. In his view, technology is more than just a collection of devices; rather, it is a revolutionary force that is changing the way people interact with one another, live, and work.

Innovation Advocate: Chris regularly participates in the tech community outside of his writing career. He attends conferences and keeps up with the latest developments in technology. His dedication to staying current guarantees that his readers get the most up-to-date and pertinent information.

Chris Amber's books are portals to a future in which technology improves our lives rather than just being books about gadgets. Having a keen sense of creativity, Chris never stops motivating and educating others, which makes him a highly sought-after contributor to the field of technical writing.

www.ingramcontent.com/pod-product-compliance
Lightning Source LLC
Chambersburg PA
CBHW031242050326
40690CB00007B/911